A Lawyer's Guide to Home Renovations

Parker Press Inc.
Briarcliff Manor, NY 10510

ISBN: 978-1-941760-02-4

For the latest information and updates to this material, check out:
http://www.reallifelegal.com/updates

A Lawyer's Guide to Home Renovations

John A. Goodman, Esq.

Real Life Legal™

Helpful Guides for Everyday Legal Matters

Parker Press Inc.

Contents

Contents

What This Book's About

Each year, hundreds of thousands of people undertake home renovation projects ranging from a few thousand dollars, to millions of dollars. Some will have lawyers review contracts for the work and others will wish they had.

While many home renovation projects turn out just fine, a good number don't! Often, having a formal, carefully reviewed contract can make a big difference. This book will help you understand key legal concepts involved in renovating your home and help you steer clear of the many pitfalls that you need to guard against. You'll get a sense of the issues that may arise in your project and whether you need a lawyer to help you navigate the process.

To get started, it's important to understand the players in a home renovation and the types of agreements which set out the rights and responsibilities of the parties. When things go wrong, contracts can help determine who is responsible for what.

It's important to have agreements in place so you can be prepared for what can be a demanding and stressful process. When your home is in upheaval, you want the other aspects of the project to be as clear and defined as possible.

Whether or not you end up using a lawyer (something we definitely recommend), you will be better prepared if you know the process, know how contracts can protect you and know what to watch out for.

Bear in mind that local custom may trump many of the legal protections that are advocated in these pages. Obviously, when in Rome, you must do as Romans do. But be sure that you verify with your attorney (or your architect, building inspector or consumer protection advocate) before you accept your contractor's word for "how things are always done around here."

Parties Involved in a Home Renovation Project

Many people have a role in taking a home renovation project from beginning to end. If you know who's involved, it makes it easier to iron out legal responsibilities and have the right people on hand for each phase of the project.

In a typical home renovation project, the primary people involved are the:

- Architect
- General contractor
- Subcontractors and suppliers
- Governmental agencies
- Lender
- Attorney

Architect

An architect is a licensed professional who assists you in planning and designing your renovation, and can make site visits during construction to verify that the contractor is doing a proper job.

General Contractor

A contractor is the person or company who takes the plans prepared by an architect and constructs the renovation project. Most states require that home improvement contractors be licensed to operate. Your state will also likely have procedures in place for you to file a complaint against your contractor for inappropriate conduct. If your contractor is not licensed in your state (assuming your state requires it), take this as a big red flag!

It's good practice to obtain at least three references for the architect and contractor under consideration. At the same time, don't place too much stock in favorable references. Some jobs go fine, some don't. Your contractor or architect can cherry-pick the projects that go well to use as references. So having a few good references doesn't necessarily imply that your contractor will do the right thing when the going gets rough!

Contact your local Department of Consumer Protection or the Better Business Bureau to find out if there are any complaints registered by homeowners who hired a contractor you have under consideration.

Subcontractors and Suppliers

Subcontractors and suppliers do the work and supply the materials for construction for specific aspects of the project. Your general contractor will order the materials and hire subcontractors to do work in their areas of specialty. Usually the subcontractors enter into separate contracts, or "purchase orders" with the general contractor, but some laborers on your project may be direct employees of the general contractor's construction company.

Governmental Agencies

Typically home renovations require building permits and other local approvals before construction begins. Your architect and contractor will have the primary interaction with your local Building Department, which issues building permits and sign-offs on the renovation work as it progresses. Aside from the Building Department, your project may also involve:

1. Separate agencies or departments that address wetlands and other environmental issues.

2. Zoning departments or an appeals board if a variance or other discretionary approval is needed.

Your architect or attorney, or both, can assist you in navigating these matters.

REAL LIFE EXAMPLE

The Goodfriends live in an 1830s antique farmhouse and have decided to tear off that ugly 1970s family room addition to add a new open kitchen and living room. The kitchen entrance is within a fifty-foot setback from the road, and the local zoning law requires a fifty-five-foot setback. The Goodfriends will need to get permission, i.e., a variance from the local zoning board, approving the setback and exterior changes to the existing structure. Their architect will assist them with the variance.

Be a Good Neighbor

It is often a good idea to let your neighbors know that you are about to undertake your renovation project. When it comes to neighbors, being considerate and helpful can sometimes make a big difference in the smooth success of your project, especially in cases where discretionary approvals are required from a government agency. You may need their okay to get a variance!

Lender

Check your mortgage to see if you need approval from your lender to do your renovation project. If you are obtaining a new construction loan to finance your project, your lender will actively review your project, and will not authorize disbursements of loan funds unless the project is on track.

Attorney

Your construction law attorney will assist you in preparing the relevant written agreements that will govern your project and can advise you as to the parties' rights when issues arise.

REAL LIFE EXAMPLE

Chester loved using his chainsaw, at any time of the day or night. Chester decided to clear some trees to make way for his renovation project, and he was having so much fun that he even removed some trees that his neighbor Freddy had asked Chester not to touch because they provided screening between their properties.

When it came time to get wetlands approval for his new entrance to the property, Freddy let it be known to the wetlands supervisor that Chester might have taken down some trees in violation of the regulations. In the end, Chester got the approvals he needed, but it cost tens of thousands of dollars in fines and extra plantings to remediate the damage to the environment.

Do I Need a Lawyer?

If you're investing a lot of time and money into a project, it's a good idea to hire a lawyer to review the contracts and make sure things go according to plan. Even if you're not really worried, it doesn't hurt to have reasonable agreements in place, in case things get upended.

Often lawyers who work in real estate get dragged into a legal battle after the parties disagree on a verbal understanding and something goes wrong. Why wait for something to go wrong to nail down the terms? Even if you hire an excellent and reputable contractor and your project goes smoothly with no unforeseen difficulties, you'll have peace of mind. Most people would prefer to be safe than sorry, so they hire a lawyer for guidance when a lot's at stake.

Your lawyer can help you take critical precautions that could save you from having a real disaster on your hands. Depending on the size of your project and how your negotiations go, hiring a lawyer will likely only add a minor fee to the cost of your project.

If you're new to home renovations and/or you are not sure about the track record of those who will be working on your home renovation, a lawyer with expertise in the field can save you a lot of headaches. Don't be penny wise and pound foolish when it comes to getting the expertise and layer of protection a lawyer provides.

The Gabriels hired Charlie as their contractor to renovate the kitchen in their home. Their neighbors had raved about Charlie, and they saw first-hand that he did excellent work. They never considered a contract or a lawyer. When Charlie asked for 50% down before he started work, they were a bit startled–but they overrode their gut instinct and paid him $7,500. After all, Charlie said he needed the funds to buy materials.

Once hired, Charlie only made one visit to sketch out plans and get an idea of cabinets and layout. But Charlie took a long time to follow up, stopped returning phone calls and never showed up to actually do the work.

What the Gabriels did not know was that Charlie was going through an ugly divorce and had cash troubles. He was taking on new jobs to get cash up front to pay for his legal fees for the divorce. In fact, he had already spent the down-payment the Gabriels gave him on other things and that is the reason he did not call back. Had the Gabriels hired a lawyer to represent them, payments would've been made as work was completed. And, odds are Charlie may have looked for an easier mark. At least the Gabriels would've been better protected and likely not out $7,500.

The Right Attorney Can Save You Money

Not only can your attorney help reduce the risk that something goes awry, he or she can also save you money. Attorneys know how to cover things in a contract that you may not have thought about.

For example, most home renovation contracts provide that the homeowner will pay for any additional costs that may occur during the renovation. For that reason, you want to make sure that anything that can be known (and lead to a possible increased cost) is known at the outset. An experienced attorney will insist on a clause in your contract that requires the contractor to represent that he isn't aware of any conditions on your property that will result in a change order which could increase the cost of the job. This means the contractor states up front that he knows of nothing that will result in an additional cost.

How does this help? Let's say there's a giant stump sitting where your new home addition is to be built. If the contractor later claims that removing the giant stump will cost you an extra $3,000, you will be able to point to the contract and say, "No way!" If the stump has been sitting there all along and this clause is in your contract, the contractor can't later say he didn't know it would add costs, because he did. As a result, you won't be hit with another $3,000 of costs.

When You Don't Need an Attorney

There *are* circumstances where you might reasonably decide that you don't need an attorney. These could include:

- Small projects involving mostly cosmetic work (painting, patching, window repair, and the like).

- Continued work with the same architect and contractor and/or with the same form of contract that was previously negotiated with the advice of an attorney.

- Projects where there are no construction loan financing, environmental or land-use issues.

- Situations where you have other relevant experience in the design, construction or legal field that adequately prepares you for most of the issues you may face.

Even if you decide not to hire an attorney to help you negotiate a deal or draw a contract for your home renovation project, don't be afraid to hire one after the project begins if things veer off course and disagreements arise. Better late than never!

You Are Always on the Hook

Even if you hire a lawyer, *you* are still responsible for all business, design and non-legal construction decisions.

- Read through your architect's agreement and construction contract, and ask questions if you don't understand something.

- Use your common sense, and don't be afraid to admit you don't know something.

- Stay on top of the progress of your renovation project, and if something doesn't seem quite right, ask your lawyer or architect.

Home Renovation Basics

If you watch enough HGTV, home renovations and their pitfalls are not new to you. But when they are your real life problems and not a reality TV program, it is a lot different.

There are many subject areas you need to be aware of when going through with a home renovation project, including:

- State law provisions

- Hidden costs

  - Change order

  - Allowance

- Payments to your contractor

State Law Provisions

Your state likely has consumer protection laws that govern home renovations. These laws may include licensing requirements, complaint procedures, rules regarding upfront deposits, and a three-day right of rescision. New York requires that consumers have a right to rescind a contract within three days if you change your mind. Make sure you're dealing with someone who knows the law and is following it.

Hidden Costs

You may think that what you ultimately pay for your project will be in line with what you initially agreed upon. But more often than not, additional costs are incurred. If your contractor encounters concealed or unforeseeable conditions, such as a huge underground boulder where a footing needs to go, he is going to submit a change order asking you for additional money to pay to have the boulder removed.

Read Proposals Carefully

Read your contractor's price proposal carefully. The bottom line price may say $40,000, but several line items may be marked as an "allowance." These can add thousands to the total price when all is said and done. It's very important to read the fine print, not just the bottom line.

Consider that you may also spend more money simply because you decided to spend more once construction is started. For example, wouldn't it be nice to have those copper gutters installed now? The contractor says he can get it done for a little less since his copper flashing guy will be on site anyway. The new gutters weren't in your original budget.

You will be tempted to spend a little more than you first intended. Count on it!

Payments to Your Contractor

Often, your contractor will ask you for an upfront "mobilization" payment to pay for materials needed to construct your renovation.

Never pay an upfront fee for materials (mobilization fee) in excess of 15% of the total cost of your renovation project.

Tips for Paying Your Contractor

- Some states even make it illegal for home renovation contractors to collect more than 10% or $1000, whichever is less, as an upfront charge.

- Never pay cash to your contractor unless you get a written paid receipt. Otherwise, it is your word against his that he's been paid.

- "Progress" payments are normally made to your contractor either bimonthly, monthly or upon completion of various phases of work.

"Retainage" is a portion of your contractor's final payment that is withheld until completion of the agreed-upon work. A **"mechanic's lien"** is a recorded claim against improved real property by a contractor, subcontractor, laborer or material supplier asserting that money is owed to them.

Tip: You should withhold a portion of every payment, called "retainage," to your contractor as an inducement to your contractor to finish the job as quickly as possible, free of mechanic's liens and in accordance with the plans. Ten percent retainage is common.

How Long Will Construction Take?

Time frames in the contract are everyone's best estimate as to how long a project will take. This depends on the contractor's other commitments, time to hire sub-contractors, order materials, get permits and the like. There may also be unforeseen circumstances which impact the time line.

- It's a good idea to specify in your contract a date by which the work must be completed. Having such a provision won't guarantee that there won't be unavoidable delays, but it may help inhibit your contractor from taking too much liberty with the time to complete your job.

- If you are especially concerned, you can include a penalty fee in the contract for construction delays. At the least it provides room for negotiation if things go wrong.

Project Scope

A project scope essentially outlines with sufficient detail the work to be done. It's very important to get this in writing, because verbal agreements often devolve into "he said, she said."

REAL LIFE EXAMPLE

Susie sat down with her contractor Harry and told him exactly what she wanted in her new addition. When it came time to draw up the contract, Harry described the scope of work as "add 1,000-square-foot addition to back of house." No architect plans or other specifics were included. Susie believed they both understood what was expected.

As construction progressed, Susie discovered in a panic that the addition didn't look anything like what she had described to Harry. But Harry did just what he said he would do—the addition was 1,000 square feet!   Susie should have included in the contract that the scope of work be based on approved architectural drawings that were referenced in the contract.

Who is Driving the Bus?

Before you sign up with your contractor, you are driving the bus. Your architect will provide you with professional guidance, but it is your budget, your tastes, your needs and desires that determine how the project moves forward. Once you are at the contract stage, your contractor is the driver.

Changing Architectural Plans: Bid vs. Final

Your contractor will submit a bid on your project using a set of preliminary drawings prepared by your architect. If the project changes at all between the drawings for the bid and the final set of drawings that are the basis of your building permit, make sure each page of the final set is correctly dated and referenced in your contract.

The contractor has been through this before and can manipulate things to squeeze money out of you, if he or she is so inclined. Make sure your construction agreement takes this reality into account.

What if the Architect or Contractor Fails to Perform?

If your architect or contractor fails to perform per your agreement, you will have no choice but to face that failure head on.

- It's essential to document the failure in writing and have records that highlight what's gone wrong.

- Hire a lawyer to assist you.

- You may need to terminate the contract and hire someone new.

If you have to fire your architect or contractor, it will very likely end up costing you more time and money to complete your project than you might first expect.

Can You Terminate a Contract?

You have the right to terminate a contract, but just how this plays out is not always predictable or pretty. If you terminate the contract because of a breach by the other side (termination "for cause"), you may get pushback as the contractor or architect tries to claim that it wasn't his or her fault.

If you terminate without asserting that there was a breach of contract, i.e., "without cause," then you may face a claim that they are entitled to all or a portion of lost profits from your project. You can protect yourself by drafting a termination clause to address this concern. This is discussed on pages 47 and 62.

What Municipal (Building, Zoning, Environmental) Regulations Govern the Project?

The answer depends on where you live and what specific issues apply to your project. If wetlands are regulated in your area and your project lies in a wetlands setback area, you will need to get approval to do your project and may need to take special steps to protect wetland areas.

Similarly, if your project lies within zoning setback lines, you may need to obtain a variance to permit you to build. Almost all municipalities will require you to obtain a building permit for your renovation, and to obtain a "certificate of occupancy" (or the equivalent) upon completion, which indicates that you are allowed to occupy your home. A certificate of occupancy indicates that construction has complied with fire, electrical and other building code requirements so that the building is safe for habitation.

It's essential that a member of your renovation team (your architect, contractor or lawyer) be familiar with permissions that are required to get government sign-offs for the work you plan. The last thing you want is to have spent time and money on a wonderful plan that cannot legally be undertaken in your town.

What Happens If There Is a Dispute?

There are many types of disputes, and depending on the severity of the issue and the terms of your agreements, differing mechanisms exist to address them.

"Mediation" is a non-binding alternative dispute resolution method in which a neutral third party, called a mediator, assists two or more parties to negotiate a settlement of their dispute. The goal is to come up with a mutually acceptable solution. In disputes

Mechanisms to Resolve Disputes

1. You work with the other side to come to an agreeable solution.

2. You enter into non-binding **"mediation."**

3. You **"arbitrate"** your dispute.

4. One party commences a lawsuit to resolve the dispute.

with your contractor, your architect will sometimes serve as the mediator.

"Arbitration" is an alternative dispute resolution method that involves streamlined procedures for submitting evidence and in which a neutral third party, called an arbitrator, makes a decision according to law and based on the evidence submitted.

- Arbitration is usually binding and the right to appeal a decision is strictly limited, such as if the decision is considered unethical or lacking sound legal basis.

- Arbitration is similar to a court trial, only it is less formal and usually quicker.

- The arbitrator is usually selected by both parties to the dispute.

Contractors and subcontractors and (depending on your state) even architects may have the right to file a "mechanic's lien" against your property if they haven't been paid for work which they claim to have properly performed on your property.

If a mechanic's lien is not removed of record, it could be a default under your mortgage loan, and will have to be cleared up before you can sell your property.

Insurance

Various types of insurance must be in place to protect you in the event of personal injury or damage to property in connection with your renovation. Insurance carried by your architect, contractor and even your homeowner's insurance needs to be reviewed to ensure you are properly protected.

Mortgage Loans

If you have a mortgage loan on your property, it should be reviewed to make sure your renovation project doesn't violate any of its terms. If you are going to obtain a construction loan to pay for the renovation, your construction lender will actively oversee your project. Construction lenders will not disburse funds unless they are satisfied that the work is proceeding properly.

Legal Agreements in Home Renovations

There are two basic legal agreements that are signed in connection with a home renovation: the architect's agreement and the construction contract.

Home renovation agreements can take many forms, from a contract scrawled on the back of an envelope to a lengthy multi-pager designed to address every conceivable issue. Absent special local rules imposed by a municipality, town or county, the parties may agree on the form of contract that they want.

That said, it's a good idea to at least start with a standard form contract recommended by a trade group, such as the American Institute of Architects (AIA), to understand all of the issues that may arise.

Construction projects usually involve several parties whose rights and responsibilities are governed by separate contracts or law.

Standard Form Contracts

The construction industry has developed a series of standard form contracts that are often the starting point for preparing a contract for your project. Lawyers representing the parties are familiar with the basic terms and prepare changes as needed.

Standard form contracts take into consideration the complexity of a construction project. The most commonly utilized and accepted standard form contracts were developed by the AIA. Some critics of the AIA documents believe the AIA forms unduly favor architects, especially when it comes to liability for mistakes made by the architect. They have a point, but the takeaway is *not* to abandon the AIA documents altogether.

Contract and agreement are terms used interchangeably by lawyers. They mean a written or verbal agreement that is intended to be legally enforceable, setting forth the rights and responsibilities of the parties.

These detailed forms cover everything—from scope of services, applications for payment, insurance, mechanic's liens, time for performance, dispute resolution and on and on. Often, it is good practice simply to have your lawyer prepare a **"rider"** to the printed AIA form, substituting alternative provisions for sections you might not want. A rider is a separate document with additional terms, to make changes or add details to the basic agreement.

Written vs. Verbal Agreements

It's essential to have a written agreement for a home renovation project. Verbal agreements are difficult to prove, and if a dispute arises, they devolve into "he said, she said." By its nature, a verbal agreement is subject to each party's memory, honesty and interpretation as to exactly what was agreed.

Who Prepares the Contract?

Most often, either the architect or the contractor provide the first draft of the agreement. But attorneys may ultimately choose to do the drafting once they have looked at the form proposed by the other party. While it can be a little more expensive to have an attorney do the initial drafting, there is the added comfort of knowing the contract has been drafted with your interests in mind.

If the contractor or architect drafts the contract, your attorney can still add a rider that specifically addresses your concerns, that are not included in the initial version.

Don't Sign a Contract 'til It's a Go!

Usually, at the time of signing, you will also be asked to make an initial payment on the contract. Changing your mind, after you are bound by your signature, can be an expensive proposition! Wait to sign until you are good to go.

Nail Down the Terms

Don't get pressured by a contractor to proceed without a written contract or to sign a bare-bones one or two page agreement lacking details. There's a lot at stake, so don't be afraid to push back. Explain that you would be more comfortable knowing that all the details (like scope of work, time for performance and payment terms) are nailed down.

State Law Applies

Agreements required for your renovation should provide that: (1) they are governed by the laws of the state in which your home is located and (2) any lawsuits will be brought in the appropriate court located in your county. This makes it easier for you to:

- Enforce provisions in your home court.

- Not be subject to an out-of-county or state jurisdiction where the architect or contractor is located, and whose laws you may not know.

- Keep your costs down if you have to litigate.

Construction Loans May Require Lender Sign-Off

If your renovation project involves a construction loan, the lender will want to review these agreements and possibly make comments on them. While the lender isn't a party to the agreements, it can condition its loan on acceptance of the construction agreements. So don't sign an agreement before you have your lender's sign-off on it. If you have an existing mortgage, you should review it to determine if any lender approvals are required to construct your renovation.

The Architect's Agreement

The AIA has standard architect agreements that are often the starting point on a project. Since the architect may be hired before the contractor, often the agreement can set the tone for many aspects of a renovation project.

The architect's agreement sets out the basic services to be performed by the architect and at what price. It should also address pricing of additional services that may be called upon in the course of your project, as well as hiring a contractor if that is to be part of the architect's job.

Typical phases of work that constitute the architect's basic services include the following:

- Schematic Design Phase

- Design Development Phase

- Construction Documents Phase

- Bidding and Negotiation Phase

- Construction Phase

Schematic Design Phase

In this initial phase, the basic scope of the project is agreed upon. With your architect, you will determine the scale of the project and explore design alternatives. **"Schematics"** or rough plans are drawn up for your approval.

Design Development Phase

During this phase, the previous schematic design work is fleshed out. You will see floor plans that show all rooms drawn to proper scale. Materials and finishes are determined. During this phase, the architect confirms that the project conforms with applicable building codes and consults with engineers if the project warrants it. Once you approve the design development plans and specifications, the architect will proceed to the construction documents phase.

Construction Documents Phase

The construction documents phase is usually the most work-intensive part of the project. This is where the detailed plans and specifications are drawn up, and they become the blueprint the contractor uses to actually build your project. The final version of these plans and specs needs to be properly referenced in your construction contract. During this phase, the architect would also prepare a set of documents to be sent to prospective contractors called "bid" documents.

Bidding and Negotiation Phase

At this stage, the architect assists you in selecting a contractor by sending the plans out to bidders with instructions regarding your requirements. The architect may even provide you with a form of agreement to be used between you and the contractor. The form may be okay, but it is still good practice to have an attorney review the contract to ensure that it covers all the bases.

Construction Phase

During the construction phase, the architect makes site visits to the project site and checks to make sure the project is being constructed according to the plans and specifications. Your agreement with the architect may also call for the architect to review and approve the contractor's applications for payment, which will require site inspections to confirm that the work has progressed as far as the contractor has claimed. If the contractor proposes a **"change order"** (described on page 59), the architect can then process it, including preparation of new drawings, if needed.

When to Pay Your Architect

An architect's fees are often paid upon completion of each phase of the work. If the architect is to develop plans and oversee work, payments are made over the course of the work.

Your architect will want to be paid a portion of fees upon completion of major sections of the work. Because the bulk of the architect's work is usually completed by the time the construction documents are done, he or she will also want to have been paid the lion's share of fees at that stage. However, you need the architect to diligently oversee construction and to make sure construction proceeds as per the plans. For that reason, we suggest you withhold substantial sums until the architect's oversight is completed.

Architect Fees Tied to Project Phase

There will be some difference between the percentage of fees your architect wants to receive and the fees you would like to pay at each stage of the project. Have your lawyer negotiate vigorously to protect your interest:

Phase	Architect Wants	You Want
Schematic Design Phase	20%	15%
Design Development Phase	30%	20%
Construction Documents Phase	30%	40%
Bidding and Negotiation Phase	5%	5%
Construction Phase	15%	20%
Total	100%	100%

Additional Architectural Services

An architect's services may change if your project changes or if changes are made to the plans. Pricing for add-ons should be considered at the time the contract is drafted.

"Additional Services" are services that may be provided by the architect, and yet are not included in the agreed-upon price for the basic services. Examples of additional services may include:

- Evaluation of bidders on behalf of the owner.

- Redesigns required by a change in requirements following the initial design.

- Services required because the owner has not promptly provided necessary information to proceed.

- Preparation for and attendance at planning board or zoning hearings regarding your project.

- Processing of change orders.

- Consultations regarding replacement of damaged work.

- Assistance with or attendance at dispute resolution hearings.

Architectural Change Orders

It is common for the architect's agreement to include the service of coordinating change orders on your behalf. An experienced architect can add a lot of value by advising you on the merits of any change order proposed by your contractor.

Who Owns the Architectural Plans?

Common sense would suggest that since you are paying your architect, you own the plans and specifications prepared for your renovation. Not necessarily! Virtually every architect agreement (the ones initially drafted by an architect) will have a clause that says that the **"instruments of service"** (plans and specifications) are copyrighted and owned by the architect.

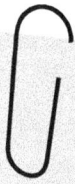

Cost Add-Ons

Additional services are usually billed at an hourly rate. To keep a handle on these overrides:

- Make sure that you do not become obligated for any additional services except those you approve in writing in advance of incurring any charges.

- Get your attorney to negotiate with the architect to shift some categories of additional services into basic services, to reduce potential overall costs under the agreement.

You are granted a **"nonexclusive license"** to use the plans, but only if you aren't in default of your agreement *and pay all sums due under your agreement!* That's where the trouble lies. What if you have a falling out with your architects halfway through the project? What if they have defaulted in their performance but argue that it wasn't their fault? You could be stuck with a design and plans you can't legally use without paying the balance on your agreement *plus* the cost of hiring a new architect to boot.

Make sure the copyright provision is modified to state that all the instruments of service are "work made for hire" and are owned by you. If the architect refuses to agree to this, at the very least, you should have the right to use the instruments of service for your project only, under any and all circumstances, without paying the architects their profit for work they haven't completed.

Indemnity and Insurance

The architect agreement most likely will include a clause to make you whole for personal injury or property damage due to the architect's negligence, and errors or omissions in performing services. This is what's known as **"indemnification."**

The risk of these problems can be covered by an insurance policy known as an "errors and omissions" policy that insures the architect for professional liability. The dollar amount of coverage will vary depending on local practices and the size of your project.

Right to Terminate Your Architect's Services

Make sure you have the right to terminate your architect's agreement *with or without cause.* This means that you can terminate even if your architect is not in breach of his or her obligations under the agreement.

If you terminate an agreement for cause, you may decide to withhold all further payments until the matter is settled. But if there has not been a performance breach, and the termination is without cause, you would pay your architect for work completed up to the date of termination.

This clause may come into play because you have had a change of circumstances, because you are having a hard time working with the architect or the architect may have breached the agreement. However, know that it is often not so easy to terminate "for cause" and including this clause means you don't have to fight it out in court to determine whether or not your architect breached a performance obligation.

The most common problem that homeowners face under their architect's agreements is that the project ends up costing much more than anticipated, due to extras that are necessary but not discussed in advance of signing the agreement.

Types of Construction Contracts

When it comes to construction contracts, the key terms are price, performance and breach. The contracts can be as simple or complicated as your concerns and take one of four basic forms.

All forms of contracts have common features such as price, time for performance and remedies for breach of contract. But as seen with architect agreements, construction contracts have unique features relevant to the type of work they cover. In fact, many of the same issues that you face with an architectural agreement will be important here too.

Types of Construction Contracts

Construction contracts take one of the following forms:

- Stipulated-Sum Contract
- Cost-Plus Contract
- Cost-Plus, with Guaranteed Maximum Price (GMP)
- Design-Build Agreement

Stipulated-Sum Contract

In a **"Stipulated-Sum Contract,"** the general contractor agrees to do the delineated scope of work for a fixed price. He will then enter into separate subcontracts with excavators, framers, plumbers, electricians, roofers, and others to do the work, also for a fixed price. The stipulated sum is the most common form of agreement and frequently the best choice.

Cost-Plus Contract

A **"Cost-Plus Contract"** is one where there isn't a fixed price at the outset. Instead, the contractor gets reimbursed for all expenses incurred in constructing the project plus his or her fee. This shifts the risk for how much the job will cost from the contractor to you. It makes sense to do this when you are under a tight time frame to complete your project and can't wait until the plans and specifications for all aspects of the work are prepared and competitively bid.

Cost Plus, with Guaranteed Maximum Price (GMP)

This contract is a cost-plus contract where some of the risk is shifted back to the contractor, who agrees to a ceiling in price that will not be exceeded unless the parties agree to a change order. Since neither the contractor nor the owner knows where the subcontractors (subs) are going to come in when their portions of work are bid, the GMP is generally going to be higher than the price of a stipulated-sum contract. Rarely will it end up being done for less than would occur under a stipulated-sum contract.

Mary and Bart are expecting twins. They're now under the gun to complete their addition well before the due date. They decide to sign a cost-plus contract with Gary even before the architect has finished the plans. This way Gary and his crew can get started with site prep and demolition. With the help of the architect, the expectant couple and their contractor are able to come up with a reasonable "Guaranteed Maximum Price (GMP)" to cap the cost of the addition. When all was said and done, Gary came in $1,000 below the GMP and the job was completed one month before the twins arrived!

Design-Build Agreement

A **"Design-Build Agreement"** can only be done by an architect or architectural firm that also does general contracting work. Essentially, both the designing of your renovation and its construction are done by one party.

- One big advantage of this kind of contract is that it streamlines the process in the interactions between the traditional architect and contractor, which can result in savings of both time and money.

- A potential disadvantage is that you lose the "checks and balances" that come from separating the design and build functions because there is no independent person to question whether the design is properly buildable, nor to verify that the construction has been properly built.

Competitive Bidding Helps You!

A chief advantage of a stipulated-sum form of contract is that it is easier to get competitive bids. Competitively bidding your final plans provides a good sense of where the market is for building your project. Plus, with this type of arrangement, contractors run the risk (not you) if their least-expensive subcontractor goes out of business, and they have to accept a much higher price for that work.

Typical Provisions in a Construction Contract

Construction contracts have standard terms that cover scope of work, progress payments, time to complete and how to handle disputes. Riders can be added for unique projects or circumstances.

A stipulated-sum contract is the most commonly used construction contract. Following are important points that will help you navigate negotiations with your contractor:

- Scope of Work

- Time for Completion of Work

- Applications for Payment

- Withholding Payment until Substantial Completion (a.k.a. Retainage)

- Final Contract Payments

- Change Orders

- Concealed Conditions

- Indemnification/Insurance

- Right to Terminate

Scope of Work

In the contract, there will be a section that lists all the relevant contract documents, and this is where you will reference the plans and specifications prepared by your architect for the project. *You need to coordinate with your architect to make sure that the referenced plans are the final ones, properly dated, and that they include all the relevant information that describes the scope of work under the contract.*

Time for Completion of Work

"Substantial Completion" is the stage in the work under the contract when the renovation can be used by you for its intended purposes. In many contracts, the contractor will look for the release of retainage at this stage, and it is also the date from which warranty periods usually run.

"Retainage" is a portion of your contractor's final payment that is withheld until completion of the agreed-upon work.

"Time Is of the Essence" means that that if your contractor fails to achieve substantial completion by a stated date, that constitutes a material breach under the contract.

It is important to state the outside date by which the contractor should achieve substantial completion. It is good practice to state that this outside date is TIME IS OF THE ESSENCE, in capital letters, so that there can be no claim that the requirement was inadvertently overlooked.

If the time for completion is especially critical to you, you can also add a **"liquidated damages"** clause to collect per diem damages for each day that the contractor is late in completing the work. Such clauses are subject to interpretation (i.e., body of case law) in each jurisdiction, so this is one area in particular where a lawyer's advice is crucial. A liquidated damage clause would provide, for example, $500 per day to the homeowner for every day the job is not completed after the "time is of the essence" date.

Applications for Payment

Your contract must spell out when your contractor is to get paid, and what documentation must be submitted for review in order to get paid. Payments can be set up with: (1) payment at specific stages of completion of the work or (2) regular draws against the contract price, such as every two weeks or once a month.

The application for payment section is important to you as well! Once you pay the contractor, he/she is obligated to pay subcontractors. The last thing you want is liens filed against your property *because your contractor decided not to pay the subcontractors.*

A **"Lien Waiver"** is a written statement by a contractor, subcontractor or supplier waiving the signor's legal right to file a lien against your property as security for a debt.

Your contractor may argue that he never gets lien waivers from subcontractors and that may be true in your area, but check with your attorney as to what is local custom.

Why You Want a Lien Waiver

If you don't get a lien waiver, you are exposed to the risk that the contractor pockets all the money and doesn't pay the subcontractors what they are owed. If this happens, the subcontractors can protect themselves by filing a lien against your property.

It is important to require that application for payment include waivers of liens from your contractor, and all major subcontractors and material suppliers (someone who furnishes materials). The right to file a lien with respect to the current payment request should also be waived by the contractor, subject to receiving such payment.

Withholding Payment Until Substantial Completion (a.k.a. Retainage)

In many contracts, retainage of 10% is withheld until substantial completion. Your contractor may ask to have retainage released for certain completed work (such as early excavation work) or to reduce retainage from 10% to 5% upon completion of a certain stage of the work. This will be dictated by local custom to some degree. Remember, it's a negotiation, and the final decision is yours.

Final Contract Payments

Final payment under the contract will be subject to additional requirements, such as the following:

- Completion of **"punch list"** items by the contractor. These include small work items that remain to be completed, as identified by you or your architect. These include spot patching and painting, leveling the flooring under the claw-foot bathtub or putting in that last strip of molding.

- Submission of final lien waivers.

- Obtaining governmental sign-offs and the certificate of occupancy (or the equivalent in your jurisdiction).

Change Orders

A **"change order"** is an agreed-upon change in the scope of work under your construction contract. It can either increase or decrease the amount of work and associated cost. Change orders arise in various circumstances, including:

- A concealed condition discovered in the progress of the work requires a change in the work.

- New design ideas occur to you along the way that you want the contractor to implement.

- The contractor discovers a deficiency in the way the architect has drawn the plans, necessitating a change in the work.

REAL LIFE EXAMPLE

The Newmans hired Walter to perform the work on their 200-square-foot addition. He was the low bidder. But his ploy to get the price back up was to hit the Newmans for change orders *after* the contract was signed.

- As the siding was removed on the west side of the house, Walter found serious rot. It wrapped around the other sides of the house too.

- The ground under the northeastern-most footing was unstable. Walter said they needed to shore it up.

- Those two weeks of off-and-on rain caused work delays and Walter lost his cement subcontractor to another job. There would be an extra charge for the replacement sub.

- The Newmans took an extra three days to choose their paint colors, so Walter had workers sitting on their hands. That was a cost increase too.

All these things resulted in change orders that increased the Newmans' final cost by 10%. Walter wasn't *entirely* dishonest about these change orders, but another contractor might have handled it differently and found ways to contain costs.

Protecting Against Hefty Change Orders

To protect against unnecessary or unfair change orders:

- Make sure that you have a good clause in your contract limiting contractor and subcontractor profit for change orders.

Change Orders Must Be in Writing!

Just as it is vitally important to have a clear, detailed construction contract for your renovation project, it is equally important that you insist that all change orders be in writing and signed. Otherwise, it's your word against the contractor's. Don't take the risk!

- Consider in advance, with your architect and lawyer, any possible areas for change orders due to concealed conditions. If necessary, do some invasive testing of walls, foundations, etc., to determine if any potential problems exist.

- Your construction contract should also set parameters as to how much you will be charged for a change order. Think of the change order like a cost-plus contract.

The contractor will bid out the work to a subcontractor and charge you an override for insurance, overhead, "general conditions" (non-staffing costs like a dumpster, temporary utilities and the like) and the contractor's fee. Your attorney or architect will be able to guide you as to what an appropriate override is, but something in the range of 11-15% is not uncommon in the New York tri-state area, for example.

REAL LIFE EXAMPLE

The Smiths hired Jerry Goodwin to be their lawyer for their renovation contract. The first change order arose when their contractor unearthed a rotted wood sill on the side of their house. Fortunately, the change-order provision in the contract capped contractor's extra fees for general conditions, insurance and profit at 12% and required that purchase orders with subs contain a similar cap. Jerry Goodwin saved the Smiths a bundle!

Protecting Against Concealed Conditions

The last thing you want is for your contractor to show up at your job and immediately hit you with a change order for a soil, rock or other condition that was somewhat concealed, but nevertheless known or suspected all along. It is a good idea to add a clause in the contract that the contractor has examined the site and that states there are no known conditions that will result in a claim for increased price or time to complete the work.

Indemnification/Insurance

Indemnification protects you against loss due to personal injury or property damage. You can require your contractor to obtain and provide suitable evidence of general liability insurance, including "products and completed operations" insurance, to be maintained for at least one year after completion of the work.

It's a good idea to inquire with your insurance agent as to how your home is insured during construction and whether additional "builder's risk" insurance needs to be obtained.

Right to Terminate

Include a clause giving you the right to fire the contractor, with or without cause. This concept was covered in the discussion of the architect's agreement on page 47.

Protecting Against Common Problems in Home Renovations

Common problems in home renovations are so common, that agreements should cover what happens if they occur. Make sure you nail down how common problems will be resolved in your contracts.

Cost overruns, time overruns, shoddy work, building code violations, the architect disappears for the summer, environmental headaches, stolen property, damage to a neighbor's property, even outright fraud: it all happens in the world of home renovations. Some of this can happen no matter what precautions you take. But some things go wrong only if you haven't been paying attention. Following are some real life examples.

Discrepancies in Bid vs. Build Plans

Bobby Bidder was the cheapest contractor among all the bidders and, besides, he was so nice. So the trusting Thompsons signed a construction contract with Bobby using Bobby's form. When it came to the arched trim at the entrance to the master bedroom, Bobby asked for more money. The Thompsons said that it was in the contract but Bobby argued that when he made his bid, the arch wasn't in the bid set of documents and just "suddenly" appeared in the final plans. Nobody could say for certain if the arch was discussed after the initial bid.

The upshot: The Thompsons stood their ground and told Bobby that it didn't matter that the bid set was different from the final set of drawings referenced in the contract; it was Bobby's job to check the final plans against the bid set. Bobby finally agreed. Tommy Thompson suspected that Bobby even knew that he had agreed upfront to the arch but was just trying to get a little extra money out of the job. We'll never know. In the end, Bobby did the right thing and completed the arch for no extra fee.

*Make sure that your final plans are properly
described in your written contract, and
make sure any significant changes from the
"bid" set of plans are signed off by
the contractor. Don't be afraid to
enforce your contract rights.*

Check for Environmental Issues at the Outset

Nate was a contractor who came recommended by friends of Patty. Patty was undertaking a complete renovation of her antique home, including installation of a finished basement under the new addition. The basement happened to abut a rock ledge. They had barely finished painting the walls when a heavy rainstorm resulted in a leak down the side of the rock ledge that destroyed the sheetrock and caused warping in the floor. Patty insisted that Nate fix his shoddy work. But Nate claimed that he was only following the architect's drawings and did everything he was supposed to do.

After nasty litigation, the parties settled. Nate was required to compensate Patty for improper work, but as part of the settlement, he never admitted that it was his fault. Patty had to hire a new contractor to finish the job, which, together with the litigation costs, added a pretty penny to the cost of Patty's project.

> *While you can't guard against every potential problem, make sure you at least check out the ones likely to arise in your neighborhood.*

If you happen to live in an area where there are known concerns that may affect the finished space or state of affairs during construction, make sure that your architect addresses the issue and this way, if any problems develop, there will be fewer questions as to who is at fault.

Monitor the Work

George and Joannie Jetsetter were so taken with Charming Charlie that they agreed to pay four million dollars to do a gut-rehab of their waterfront mansion. The Jetsetters were around for the first part of the work and were impressed with the verve of Charlie's workers as they tore off the old worn shingles to make way for the new roof. Then off the Jetsetters went to spend the summer in the Hamptons with friends. Each time Charlie made a request for an advance, he included a glowing report about how well things were going at the old homestead. The Jetsetters just loved his writing style!

The Jetsetters had arranged to have their mail forwarded by the local post office. It really put a damper on their summer vacation to receive a *notice of condemnation* from their town building department! Apparently, after Charlie opened up the roof to the elements, he took off for parts unknown and *continued to collect payments* from the Jetsetters without doing any work!

If you can't be present during construction, make sure someone can be there to monitor progress of the work. Also, make sure your agreements with your architect and contractor include the requirement that your architect inspect and sign off on applications for payment at each stage of completed work.

Have an "End Date" in Your Contract

Tom and Tammy Tanner were so excited that Conner Construction made such an affordable bid to put in two new bathrooms and a septic system. They quickly signed Carter Conner's two-page contract. Since they were only replacing the bathrooms and not touching the rest of the house, the Tanners made no plans to move out. They could use the porta-potty outside in the meantime. Conner Construction showed up right on time and completed the demolition phase of the project lickety-split. That was in October.

Come November 10th, Tammy noticed that not much had happened with the project since the first week. Carter Conner was apologetic, saying that his septic guy had been pulled onto a much bigger job, but that he promised he would be over soon.

By December, the kids started complaining that the outdoor porta-potty seat was very cold and they wished they didn't have to go to Grandma's to take a shower. The septic guy was very polite when he apologetically explained that the ground was frozen and they would have to wait until the spring thaw to finish the job.

By April, the septic system was finally working and new bathrooms were complete and beautiful, just like Carter Conner promised. Only many months late!

Make sure your written contract requires your contractor to perform the work by a certain date. If you have no better options and choose to remain in part of your home while construction is ongoing, your agreement should require that necessary amenities are addressed first! Keep at least one functional bathroom at all times!

Do Your Due Diligence: Get Meaningful References

Rudy submitted three great references to Joe and Dolly Parson, including one from the Petersons down the road. Bob Peterson even told the Parsons that he had gotten so chummy with Rudy that he would often ask Rudy to pick up pizza before he swung by the house to check on the day's progress. Rudy seemed like such a nice guy. The Parsons didn't check other references after talking with Bob Peterson.

The Parson's house was an 1830s antique with a dirt basement. Their addition in the back was going to have a new basement, with a cement floor. The floor was going to be a good two feet further below grade than the old dirt basement.

When it came time to excavate for the new basement, Rudy seemed pretty sure that he could pull out the boulders that supported the foundation under the old part of the house and then put in the cinderblock wall between the old and new basement. How hard could it be?

Dolly Parson was upstairs when she heard a sudden "CRACK!" The floor shifted. Water started coming through the wall where the sink was once located. Dolly screamed.

Rudy insisted that there was no way he could have known that the existing house would be destabilized when he ripped out the underpinning. The architect and the architect's engineer disagreed. After a nasty fight, the Parsons and Rudy reached a settlement, parted ways and a new contractor came in to shore up the old house and finish the renovation.

It goes without saying that people will give you references who will say good things. But take the time to get references, consider them carefully and ask what went right and/or wrong with the job. There can be a lot at stake and "being a nice guy" isn't what it's about. Getting the job done properly, on budget and on time is what matters most.

Get a Scope of Work with an Estimate

Mark was Jean Anderson's friend. He had done work on her house before, his work was good and in their first project together he came in right on budget. The Andersons were in the final stages of their interior home renovation and they thought they had enough savings to re-do the mudroom. Jean approached Mark and told him she wanted to spend about $5,000 on the mudroom. She gave him the particulars and asked if he could do it for that price.

Mark responded, "Yeah, that sounds about right."

About halfway through the mudroom work Jean checked in with Mark and asked, "Are we still on track at $5,000?"

Mark responded, "Well, it's gonna be more."

Now they were in the thick of it. As the work continued, Jean kept asking what it was going to cost and Mark kept putting her off. In the end, the mudroom upgrade cost the Andersons double the original estimate!

_____

An estimate without a scope of work is fraught with things that can go wrong. Make sure that your contractor gives you a written estimate that also details the scope of work. If things go wrong, you want to know the outside limit of your liability and you want the contractor to share the risk for a shoddy estimate.

_____

Concluding Thoughts

Renovating your home is exciting and can be fun. But it can also be stressful. Get good contracts in place and protect yourself if things veer off course, which can happen with the best laid plans.

Home renovations often take a lot longer and cost more than you first imagine. If you are approaching the project with a significant other, there may be strain from it all at times. Yet on the far side of all that planning, discussing, and resolving renovation issues is the home improvement you dreamed of!

With the information on these pages, you can approach your home renovation project with greater confidence, and know how to avoid many of the pitfalls that befall others. Make sure to have a written contract that details everything that you know can come up, that you can plan for. If you have reached an agreement with your contractor on what it should cost and when it will be completed, why wouldn't you write it down in detail? If that's a problem for him or her, think twice! Not putting your agreement in writing rarely benefits anyone but your contractor.

Think about it. How much extra work is it, really, to put down in writing exactly what has been agreed to? Most contracts begin as form documents. If your contractor has been in business for any length of time, it should be easy for her to generate the written agreement.

Most contractors will drop their insistence on working without a written agreement as soon as they know you have an attorney representing you.

Should you have a dispute with your general contractor (or architect), you should not hesitate to turn to your lawyer for advice as to the rights of the parties under your contract.

Renovation Checklist:

☐ Check contractor references.

☐ Verify that your contractor is licensed.

☐ Check if the contractor has complaints filed against him.

☐ Draw up complete and accurate plans with your architect.

☐ Include those plans in a formal contract.

☐ Pay attention to the difference in "bid" vs. "build" architectural plans.

☐ Listen to that small inner voice that alerts you when something doesn't seem right.

☐ Pay attention to your project as it progresses.

☐ Address problems, troubles or misunderstandings right away.

☐ Get an attorney involved to protect your interests.

Glossary

Additional Services: Services that may be provided by the architect, and yet are not included in the agreed-upon price for the basic services.

Allowance: An item in the contract price that hasn't been finally determined and thus the price for that item remains open.

American Institute of Architects (AIA): Publishes standard form agreements used by architects.

Arbitration: An alternative dispute resolution method that involves streamlined procedures for submitting evidence and in which a neutral third party called an arbitrator makes a decision according to law and based on the evidence submitted.

Certificate of Occupancy: A document issued by a local building or zoning authority which indicates that construction has complied with fire, electrical and other building code requirements so that the building is safe for habitation.

Change Order: A written or oral agreement between you and your contractor to change some aspect of the scope of work under your construction contract.

Competitive Bidding: Architectural plans prepared for "bid" are circulated to contractors to get bids on a project.

Cost-Plus Contract: Construction contract that doesn't fix price at the outset. Instead contractor gets reimbursed for all expenses incurred in constructing the project plus his or her fee.

Design-Build Agreement: Renovation contract entered with an architectural firm that also does general contracting work.

Guaranteed Maximum Price (GMP): Type of construction contract which shifts risk to the contractor by establishing a ceiling price which cannot be exceeded without agreement on a change order.

Indemnification: A clause to make you whole for personal injury or property damage due to another's negligence, errors or omissions in performing services.

Instruments of Service: Generally refers to an architect's plans and specifications.

Lien Waiver: A written statement by a contractor, subcontractor or supplier waiving the signor's legal right to file a lien against your property as security for a debt.

Liquidated Damages: Amount of per diem damages for each day that the contractor is late in completing the work.

Litigation: A lawsuit or proceeding in a court of law presided over by a judge.

Mechanic's Lien: A recorded claim against improved real property by a contractor, subcontractor, laborer or material supplier asserting that money is owed to them. They will affect title transfers if not resolved.

Mediation: Non-binding alternative dispute-resolution method in which a neutral third party called a mediator assists two or more parties to negotiate a settlement of their dispute.

Punch List: List of small work items that require completion, as compiled by contractor and home renovator.

Glossary

Rider: A separate legal document with additional terms. They are used to make changes or add details to the basic agreement.

Retainage: A portion of your contractor's final payment that is withheld until completion of the agreed-upon work.

Schematics: Rough plans drawn up by an architect for a project.

Scope of Work: Detailed description of the work to be done. Deviations or changes from the original scope of work may be subject to additional fees and costs.

Stipulated-Sum Contract: Contractor agrees to do the delineated scope of work for a fixed price. Contractor hires workers/sub-contractors for a fixed price.

Substantial Completion: The stage in the work under the contract when the renovation can be used by you for its intended purposes.

Time Is of the Essence: Often a contract clause which provides that if your contractor fails to achieve *substantial completion* by a stated date, that constitutes a material breach under the contract. Should be written in the contract with capital letters, i.e., TIME OF THE ESSENCE, so there can be no claim that the requirement was inadvertently overlooked.

About the Author

John A. Goodman, Esq.

John A. Goodman, Esq., is a commercial real estate attorney in solo practice in Westchester County, New York. He specializes in real estate, construction law, leasing, general contract and corporate law and is a certified mediator. Mr. Goodman graduated *summa cum laude* from Bucknell University and received his J.D. from Columbia Law School. He is licensed to practice in New York

About Real Life Legal™

Parker Press Inc., the publisher of Real Life Legal™ creates plain language consumer information on legal, tax, business and financial subjects. Taking aim at info overload and legalese, Parker Press Inc. launched Real Life Legal™ in 2014. Real Life Legal™ provides practical advice, written by lawyers, to help people understand how the law works. Our goal is to provide solid, easy-to-understand information so *you* can decide whether it makes sense to hire a lawyer. Real Life Legal™ wants you to be prepared.

Available Titles

Bankruptcy Basics: Chapter 7 and Chapter 13
Marina Ricci, Esq.

Business Owners Startup Guide
Susan G. Parker, Esq. and Lynne Williams, Esq.

Elder Law: Legal Planning for Seniors
Susan G. Parker, Esq. and Maria B. Whealan, Esq.

Employee's Guide to Discrimination and Termination
Joanne Dekker, Esq.

Estate Planning: A Road Map for Beginners
Susan G. Parker, Esq. and Maria B. Whealan, Esq.

Filing a Homeowner's Claim: Natural Disaster or Not
Dawn Snyder, Esq.

A Lawyer's Guide to Home Renovations
John A. Goodman, Esq.

Available Titles (Continued)

Planning for Pets: Trusts, Leash Laws and More
Joanne Dekker, Esq.

Planning for Your Special Needs Child
Amy Newman, Esq.

Special Needs Education: Navigating for Your Child
Lynne Williams, Esq.

U.S. Veterans: Your Rights and Benefits
Maria B. Whealan, Esq.
with Paul M. Goodson, Esq.

What to Do When Someone Dies
Susan G. Parker, Esq.

You've Been Arrested: Now What?
Maryam Jahedi, Esq.

Notes

Notes

Notes

Notes

Notes

Notes

Notes

Notes

Notes

Notes

Notes

Notes

Notes

Notes

Notes

Notes

Notes

Notes

Notes

Notes

Notes

Notes